COVER TO COVER

BIBLE **STUDY**
7 SESSIONS FOR SMALL GROUP
AND PERSONAL USE

1 Timothy

HEALTHY CHURCHES - EFFECTIVE CHRISTIANS

CWR

D1422213

Christine Platt

Published 2004 by CWR, Waverley Abbey House, Waverley Lane, Farnham, Surrey GU9 8EP, UK. Registered Charity No. 294387. Registered Limited Company No. 1990308. Reprinted 2008, 2010, 2016.

For a list of National Distributors, visit www.cwr.org.uk/distributors

Unless otherwise indicated, all Scripture references are from the Holy Bible: New International Version (NIV), copyright © 1973, 1978, 1984 by the International Bible Society.

Concept development, editing, design and production by CWR.
Front cover image: Roger Walker.
Printed in the UK by Linney Group

ISBN: 978-1-85345-291-8

Contents

Introduction

This first-century letter is highly relevant for today's Church. Although it was addressed to Timothy to help him in his leadership of the Ephesian church, its themes of sticking to the pure truth, being alert to false teaching, church organisation, and living lives that reflect Christ are contemporary issues that face thinking Christians whether or not in church leadership.

And yet the world has changed dramatically since Paul wrote this letter. None of us live any longer in the culture of first-century Asia. We need to work out what are timeless principles as opposed to cultural practices and see how they apply to us today. To responsibly interpret this letter demands discernment and wisdom. It also deals with some controversial issues regarding the position of women in church, which can be a very emotive subject for both men and women.

We have a vital need for the Holy Spirit to be our Teacher as we delve into this letter (John 16:13). We need to be brave enough to put aside our prejudices, come afresh to Scripture and be open to learn, to evaluate, to pray and to seek God's Word for us in this twenty-first century.

Paul is generally acknowledged to be the author of this letter which forms part of the Pastoral Letters – 1 and 2 Timothy and Titus.

Timothy was born in Lystra (modern Turkey) to a Greek father and a Jewish Christian mother (Acts 16:1). He had joined Paul on his travels and was a valued co-worker (Phil. 2:19–23). When Paul was released from his imprisonment in Rome (c. AD 60–62, Acts 28:30) he resumed his travels and left Timothy in charge of the church in Ephesus (1 Tim. 1:3). When it seemed to Paul that he might not return very soon he decided to write (probably c. AD 63–65), and give Timothy some further instructions and encouragement (1 Tim. 3:14–15). The close relationship between Paul and Timothy is evident in the way Paul addresses him: 'My true son in the faith' (1 Tim. 1:2) and 'my dear son' (2 Tim. 1:2). Possibly Paul had led Timothy to Christ.

Some pioneers in ministry excel in getting new ventures off the ground but are no good at maintaining an interest in them once they've gone on to pastures new. Paul, by contrast, combines the gift of apostle (pioneer) – going where no one had gone before – and pastor – maintaining contact with churches he had established and making sure they had good leadership.

One of Paul's reasons for writing was that the Ephesian church was under attack from false teachers. They advocated an early form of Gnosticism which taught that the spirit was all good, and the material world was all evil. One teaching that flowed from this was that salvation was an escape from the (evil) body and you needed some special knowledge (Greek *'gnosis'*) in order to be saved. This was like a red rag to a bull to Paul. He insists on the uniqueness of faith in Christ for salvation. 'Christ Jesus came into the world to save sinners' (1:15) and 'there is one... mediator between God and men, the man Christ Jesus' (2:5).

Extreme asceticism also came out of the belief that the material world is all evil, thereby leading people to forbid marriage and the eating of certain foods (4:1–5). Paul was a passionate campaigner for the believer's freedom to enjoy all that God had so generously given.

Another false teaching was legalistic Judaism, where teachers were including Jewish myths and 'building up endless, far-fetched, fictitious stories based on obscure

genealogical points' (NIV Study Bible note on 1:3–7).
The result of these was controversy rather than building
up the people of God.

Paul does not attempt to find a way to accommodate any
of this. He refutes it firmly and urges Timothy to do the
same. Guard the gospel in its purity – faith in Christ alone
– that is his resounding motto.

Today we encounter different false teachings, such as
the prosperity gospel, New Age philosophies, blurring of
moral standards, to name a few. It is of vital importance
that we correctly handle the word of truth (2 Tim. 2:15)
so that we are quick to discern error in ourselves and in
those in positions of influence. Today's Christians have
the responsibility to guard the pure gospel to pass on to
succeeding generations just as those who've gone before,
like Paul and Timothy, have preserved it for us.

There is a severity in Paul in this letter. He is very tough
on false teachers, but is gentle and compassionate towards
Timothy. He encourages him to look after his health and
not to let people look down on him because of his youth.
(In those days this meant up to 40 years old!)

Paul's love for Christ also surges up throughout this letter.
When talking about the gospel and his own experience
of God's mercy, he explodes in praise to the One who
makes it all possible (1:17; 6:15–16).

This is a good balance to keep in mind as you study.
In the midst of wrestling to identify false teachings and
coping with knotty problems of church organisation, let's
also aim to deepen in our love and devotion to Christ
and see Him through these pages.

'Now to the King eternal, immortal, invisible, the only
God, be honour and glory for ever and ever. Amen' (1:17).

WEEK 1

God is Listening

Opening Icebreaker

Have verses on prayer written on cards (see Leader's Notes for suggestions). Each group member takes a card and reads out the verse. Any group member could share any experience related to that verse.

Bible Readings

- 1 Timothy 1:12–17; 2:1–8; 6:13–16
- Ephesians 3:20

Opening Our Eyes

If anyone had an excuse to be too busy to pray it was Paul. He worked tirelessly for the gospel and spent himself in evangelism and teaching, doing all he could to build up God's Church. He experienced spectacular success, but also spectacular opposition – from enemies outside the Church, and also from within, who sought and succeeded to undermine his hard work (1:18–20).

He had people to talk with, meetings to attend, letters to write, journeys to make, many challenges. It would have been understandable if he had decided to leave the responsibility of prayer to the older women in the church and just got on with 'the business'.

Many committed Christians also feel busy and are perhaps over-stretched. Solid, thoughtful prayer can get squeezed out and we grab a few moments to talk with God before the next activity or before we fall asleep at night. Then another sermon comes along that stimulates us to unearth the priority of prayer once again and we start off with great intentions. Before we know what's happened, 'life' crowds in once more, and so it goes on.

Yet it seems that however busy Paul was, praise and prayer permeated his life.

What can we learn from him to help us get off the rollercoaster of our up and down prayer lives?

Recognition of need
Paul reminds himself and his readers of what he was before Christ took hold of him – a blasphemer, persecutor, violent man, worst of sinners (1:13,16). He recognised his constant need of God's mercy and how Christ had made it possible for him to receive that mercy. As he allowed this truth to grip his mind it inevitably led

him to praise. He just can't seem to get over the fact that God has been so kind to such an undeserving soul.

Lift mind and heart in praise

Paul doesn't actually exhort Timothy to praise God in this letter, but praise just pops out in his writing. As mentioned before, the source of praise is recognising all that God is and all He has done. Focusing on these truths when we come to prayer will build our faith to pray big worshipful prayers.

Recognition of the enemy

Paul knew that Satan was the source of the opposition (4:1). Sometimes in church disputes it seems that our fellow Christians become the enemy, but we need to attack the true enemy behind all opposition.

Use spiritual weapons

Paul taught that spiritual forces require spiritual weapons that 'have divine power to demolish strongholds' (2 Cor. 10:4). Ten thousand meetings and endless discussions will not defeat spiritual opposition. The fall of the Berlin Wall and the lifting of the Iron Curtain were not accomplished by crack troops with rocket launchers. People prayed and God answered.

Perseverance

In the parable of the persistent widow in Luke 18, Jesus urges us to always pray and not give up. The story is told of a family in North Africa who lived next door to a bakery. Day after day the machinery gave off small vibrations against their adjoining wall. There was no indication of a problem until one day the wall suddenly collapsed! We have no way of knowing what God is doing under the surface of problems before the cracks start to appear, but by faith we believe that He is in the process of 'demolishing strongholds'.

Discussion Starters

1. What picture does Paul paint of Christ and of God the Father in these verses?

_____

_____

_____

_____

2. What is Paul's heart attitude towards God?

_____

_____

_____

_____

3. How might he have arrived at these convictions about Christ?

_____

_____

_____

_____

4. How did these convictions about Christ and God the Father help him in his prayer life?

_____

_____

_____

_____

5. Why is it necessary for us to have Christ as mediator?

_____

_____

_____

_____

6. How would you encourage someone who felt too unworthy to pray?

_____

_____

_____

_____

7. What would you say to someone who had given up praying because God hadn't answered?

_____

_____

_____

_____

8. Paul emphasises the importance of thankfulness. Why do you think this is?

_____

_____

_____

_____

9. What helps you to praise God?

_____

_____

_____

_____

10. How can you go deeper in prayer, both as an individual and in your group?

_____

_____

_____

_____

Personal Application

Satan trembles when he sees Christians on their knees. Paul knew that these false teachings would destroy the church, but teaching alone would not correct the problem, prayer was vital. It is impossible to know how much time Paul spent in prayer. He no doubt prayed as he walked and worked; it was the very breath he breathed.

He also urged the church to pray for those in authority. It is much easier to criticise governments and global organisations than take the time to seriously pray for them. How can you incorporate prayer into your day in a more meaningful way? Do you need to reassess your priorities so you can pray privately and also with other Christians?

Paul's high view of God led him to pray audacious prayers. Are your prayers king-sized? How can you grow in this area?

Seeing Jesus in the Scriptures

Jesus also craved time with His Father and took time out from hectic days to be alone to pray (Mark 1:35). He prayed short prayers (John 11:41) and longer prayers (John 17; Luke 6:12). He taught many things about prayer – one of the most important and radical is that we pray to a God who is our Father (Matt. 6:9). This mighty, holy, majestic, all-powerful and all-knowing King, for whom nothing is impossible, is our Father. We can come to Him and know we are loved as precious children and that 'no good thing does he withhold from those whose walk is blameless' (Psa. 84:11).

WEEK 2

Watch Out! False Teachers About!

Opening Icebreaker

The following verses have been deliberately misquoted.
Discuss what false teaching might flow from them.

1. For God so loved the world that he gave his only Son
so that everyone would have eternal life (from John 3:16).

2. If we confess our sins and feel really bad about them
for weeks, he is faithful and just and will forgive our sins
and purify us from all unrighteousness (from 1 John 1:9).

3. Most Scripture is God-breathed and useful for teaching,
rebuking, correcting and training in righteousness (from
2 Tim. 3:16).

Bible Readings
- 1 Timothy 1:3–11; 4:1–8; 6:3–5
- 1 John 4:1–6

Opening Our Eyes

When people are being trained to recognise counterfeit bank notes they don't study forgeries, they constantly handle the real stuff. The more familiar they are with genuine notes, the quicker they'll be at picking up the dud ones. When seeking to identify false teachers, we need to have the Word of God clearly as our 'gold standard'.

Paul had a thorough knowledge of the Jewish Scriptures. He had been a Pharisee and obeyed the law to the letter (Phil. 3:4–6). When Jesus intervened in his life in that dramatic encounter on the Damascus road, his understanding of God's Word was transformed by the revelation of the One to whom the Old Testament points (Acts 9).

Paul was convinced of the vital importance of believing the truth. 'All Scripture is God-breathed and is useful for teaching, rebuking, correcting and training in righteousness, so that the man of God may be thoroughly equipped for every good work' (2 Tim. 3:16–17). What we believe dictates our actions. However sincere we are in believing a lie, our sincerity can never make it true (Prov. 14:12). An anorexic person truly believes she looks fat even though to her grieving friends and family she is painfully thin. Unless the sufferer changes her belief it will eventually destroy her.

Right from the beginning of human history Satan has sought to undermine people's belief in God and the truth of His Word. He put another spin on what God said to Eve and she fell for it with catastrophic consequences (Gen. 3). Satan's tactics have not changed. He still aims to sidetrack us from the truth.

The Early Church was constantly attacked by false teachings (see Introduction) as it strove to preserve the fundamental truth: salvation by faith in Christ alone and not through the law. Paul even had to oppose the revered apostle Peter when he wavered in his convictions (Gal. 2:11–16).

When an individual or a group breaks away from the established Church or just decides to set up a religion for themselves, there are three basic tests to ascertain whether their teaching is of God or not:

a) The honour given to Jesus Christ
Some groups acknowledge Him as a teacher or a prophet, but not as the Son of God, sharing a oneness with God the Father; whereas Scripture is unequivocal. God acknowledges Jesus as His Son (Heb. 1:5). Jesus claimed: 'I and the Father are one' (John 10:30).

b) Their attitude towards the Bible
Some groups use the Bible but also have another book or writings to which they refer and, for them, these writings carry equal authority with the Bible. There are dire warnings about this in Revelation 22:18–19.

c) How mankind can receive salvation
As in Paul and Timothy's time, some groups today claim you need something else apart from faith in Christ alone. Some say living a good life is sufficient. Others say you need Christ and good works. Meditation and self-denial are also seen as ways to approach God. The Bible states clearly that we can do nothing to earn our way to God (Eph. 2:8–9). Jesus is the way (John 14:6).

It is important to distinguish between basic tenets of faith – who is Jesus, how we can be saved, the place of God's Word. These are clearly non-negotiable; whereas there are many other issues over which Christians can have different views, eg the Sabbath, drinking alcohol, smoking, which should not be allowed to cause division (1 Cor. 8).

Discussion Starters

1. How does Paul describe false teachers (4:1–2)?
   _____
   _____
   _____
   _____
   _____

2. What is the result of false teaching?
   _____
   _____
   _____
   _____
   _____

3. How does Paul describe the false teaching? What are some current false teachings you are aware of?
   _____
   _____
   _____
   _____
   _____

4. Who or what is the source of these teachings?
   _____
   _____
   _____
   _____
   _____

5. How should we respond to these teachers and their teaching?
   _____
   _____
   _____
   _____

6. The warning is given in 1 Timothy 4:1 that 'some will abandon the faith and follow deceiving spirits'. How can we guard ourselves from being wrongly influenced?

_____

_____

_____

_____

_____

7. Leaving aside the non-negotiable truths as mentioned in Opening Our Eyes, what other issues have you found that Christians disagree on?

_____

_____

_____

_____

_____

8. What principles should we use to maintain unity in these circumstances?

_____

_____

_____

_____

_____

Personal Application

Sometimes false teachers can become very popular. Their charisma and appealing message bring the crowds in, which can occasionally be interpreted as God blessing the work. Unfortunately experience later shows there to be rottenness at the core. 'By their fruit you will recognise them' (Matt. 7:16).

Let's not be fooled by popularity. Let's be sure that the message is true and the speaker 'walks the talk'. Our responsibility in matters spiritual, whether we hear it in church, on the radio or read it in a book, is to follow the good example of the Bereans who 'received the message with great eagerness and examined the Scriptures every day to see if what Paul said was true' (Acts 17:11).

Seeing Jesus in the Scriptures

Jesus was deeply upset about the false teaching that He encountered during His earthly life. He called the Pharisees 'blind guides' in Matthew 23:16. He denounced them for placing a wrong emphasis on minor issues while neglecting the biggies (Matt. 23:23–24).

In Matthew 5:17 Jesus says: 'Do not think that I have come to abolish the Law or the Prophets; I have not come to abolish them, but to fulfil them.' 'Jesus fulfilled the Law in the sense that He gave it its full meaning. He emphasised its deep underlying principles and total commitment to it rather than mere external acknowledgement and obedience' (NIV Study Bible).

If we stay close to Jesus, we need not fear being led astray. He promised that His Holy Spirit would lead us into all truth (John 16:13).

WEEK 3

Use Your Gifts

Opening Icebreaker

Play this matching game. Which gifts go with the following individuals?

• Paul (1 Tim. 2:7)	Leadership
• Dorcas (Acts 9:36)	Serving
• Timothy (1 Tim. 4:11)	Miracle-worker
• Anna (Luke 2:36)	Teaching
• Elijah (1 Kings 17)	Prophet
• Elisha (2 Kings 4:32–37)	Healer
• David (1 Sam. 16:1, 13)	Apostle

Bible Readings
• 1 Timothy 1:18–20; 4:6–16; 6:12–14,20–21
• Romans 16:6–8
• 1 Corinthians 12:7–11

Opening Our Eyes

Timothy didn't have an easy assignment. Ephesus was a major city where the great goddess Artemis was worshipped (Acts 19:23–41). 'The Ephesian Artemis had taken on the characteristics of Cybele, the mother goddess of fertility worshipped in Asia Minor and served by many prostitute priestesses' (NIV Study Bible). Sorcery and magical incantations were rife (Acts 19:18–19). This was a difficult spiritual environment for a young man charged with guiding the fledgling church. Timothy was much in need of encouragement and guidance from his good friend and mentor.

Having warned him about false teachers, Paul states the positive action: 'Fight the good fight' (1:18); 'Command and teach these things' (4:11); 'Guard what has been entrusted to your care' (6:20).

I wonder if Timothy felt a bit inadequate for this role; Paul was a hard act to follow. Paul reminds him that God had placed him there. Prophecies had been made about him (1:18); he had received a gift (4:14). With God's help he could do it. His main job seems to have been to teach the truth and urge people to believe and obey (4:13).

God can only develop gifts in us as we use them, and that gives an opportunity for them to be affirmed by other mature godly leaders. 'Do not neglect your gift,' Paul urges. Timothy had to bravely take on these responsibilities and as he began to serve, God began to give him the resources he needed. Gifts are not developed in us if we stay within our comfort zone.

It seems that Timothy's leadership had been called into question (4:12) which would make it doubly difficult for him to step out in faith.

What practical resources did Timothy have to help him fulfil his task?

- Old Testament Scriptures
- Letter from Paul
- Memories and experience from his missionary travels.

Today in the developed world we are bountifully supplied with a myriad of resources. Bibles in every conceivable version, study books, podcasts, videos, radio and television programmes as well as learning from our own pastors and teachers. Opportunities abound for us to use and develop our gifts.

Timothy's generation was establishing a whole new order of God's people – Jews and Gentiles worshipping together. They had no organisational structures to lean on, no church buildings; everything they did was new. It must have been thrilling to be a pioneer like that, but also scary. They were laying a foundation and, as we all know, if the foundation is shaky the building will eventually fall down. What a huge responsibility on this sometimes sickly, possibly fearful young man's shoulders.

But God had called him and Paul had confidence in him. When Paul wrote his second letter to him, possibly four to six years after the first one, Timothy was still in Ephesus and, as far as we can ascertain, still doing a good job.

Paul's wise words in 4:16 are salutary for us all: 'Watch your life and doctrine closely.' God's workers can become so busy caring for others that they neglect themselves and their own spiritual growth. The consequences of this can be catastrophic. We can only teach others what we have truly learned ourselves. God has to work in us and then He can work through us (Phil. 2:12–13).

Discussion Starters

1. What might have been an appropriate job description for Timothy's role?
The Church in Ephesus seeks:

_____

_____

_____

_____

_____

2. What qualifications, gifts and experience would be helpful for a person filling that role? What qualifications, gifts and experience did Timothy have to offer?

_____

_____

_____

_____

_____

3. What might have been the most difficult parts of Timothy's job?

_____

_____

_____

_____

_____

4. What do you think helped him to persevere?

_____

_____

_____

_____

5. How might Timothy have identified his gift?

_____

_____

_____

_____

_____

6. Why does the Holy Spirit give gifts?

_____

_____

_____

_____

_____

7. What happens when gifts are not used?

_____

_____

_____

_____

_____

8. Have you identified your gift? What steps can you take to identify your gift and use it more fully?

_____

_____

_____

_____

_____

Personal Application

As we've seen, the Holy Spirit gives gifts to Christians. All of them are vital in order that the Church should flourish and reach her full potential as an effective instrument to bring glory to God in this world. It's tempting to think that the up-front gifts are more important, but Scripture does not allow us to entertain that thought. We should neither belittle our gifts nor over-emphasise them.

Our responsibility is to identify them and use them to the full, and not compare ourselves with others. In the seasons of life that we encounter, there may be times when our gifts are used in a different context. Circumstances of life will determine how our gifts will be best used. For example, parents of small children and carers of elderly or sick family members may find their gifts are used mainly in the home. But whatever our circumstances we must use these gifts; they should never be shelved waiting for that perfect opportunity.

Seeing Jesus in the Scriptures

Jesus' final words to His disciples before ascending into heaven were: 'But you will receive power when the Holy Spirit comes upon you' (Acts 1:8). The Holy Spirit gives gifts and He is also the source of the power we need to use those gifts rightly. A light bulb is a perfectly equipped item, but its potential cannot be unleashed until it is switched on. The gifts are within us and the power is available. Let's honour Jesus by using our gifts fully in His service by His Holy Spirit's power.

WEEK 4

Walk the Talk

Opening Icebreaker

Word associations:
Read out the fruit of the Spirit (Gal. 5:22–23) one by one, and ask each person in the group to write down the first word that comes into their minds relating to that quality. Share around at the end.

Bible Readings

- 1 Timothy 2:8–10; 6:1–2,11
- Matthew 7:20
- John 15:4–5,8
- Galatians 5:22–23
- 1 John 2:6

Opening Our Eyes

One of the accusations flung at Christians is 'Hypocrite! You say one thing and do another!' What the unbelieving world is looking for is men and women with integrated lives – that when we talk of a God of love and compassion we show it in our actions. When we speak of our God who gives joy and peace, our faces show it. When we say 'God so loved the world' we put flesh and blood onto that and reveal deep concern and sacrificial generosity for those in other countries, particularly the hurting and needy.

What image do people get of God by looking at our lives?

The image often given of Christians by the media is of somewhat irrelevant figures of fun. Unless unbelievers have Christians as friends, work colleagues, family, their convictions about God's people are formed by what's on that mighty powerful medium, the TV. We have an uphill struggle to get out there and show what real Christians are like. There is no point having a seeker service if there are no seekers there.

I constantly hear testimonies of people being drawn to Christ by seeing someone's godly character – 'I experienced real love through my friend.' The well-executed gospel message might be the final link in the chain but the groundwork is done by living letters of Christ (2 Cor. 3:3).

The qualities that reflect God are called 'fruit of the Spirit'. Fruit needs nourishment to grow and as we stay close to Christ, the Vine (John 15:5), He, by His Spirit, forms His fruit in us.

Fruit grows slowly, so we need to be patient with ourselves when we fail. Praying for patience will inevitably bring irritating circumstances our way.

Patience only grows as we experience the need for it. Love grows as we encounter the unlovely. Joy comes when we look beyond our current circumstances to the true joy found in Christ. This rather old-fashioned poem by Edgar Guest expresses this concept very well.

I'd rather see a sermon than hear one, any day,
I'd rather one should walk with me than merely tell
   the way;
The eye's a better pupil and more willing than the ear,
Fine counsel is confusing, but example's always clear,
And the best of all the preachers are the men who
   live their creeds,
For to see good put in action is what everybody
   needs.

Sermons we see, Edgar Guest

It can be devastating to be found wanting in our Christian behaviour. We can feel that we've blown it forever, particularly with non-Christians. But forgiveness is always available. We need to confess to God and receive His forgiveness. I've found that also saying sorry to the person involved leads to really interesting conversations. People are amazed someone would bother to apologise to them. God, in His mercy and wisdom, has turned my failure into something positive.

Physical appearance is also covered in 1 Timothy 2:9–10. The word 'modest' means 'decent and orderly'. The way we dress needs to enhance the cause of Christ and not detract from it. In the past Christians were generally dowdy and Christ was seen to be a killjoy and rather boring. It's great to follow fashion as long as we're not enslaved to it and our appearance is still decent and orderly. Our motivation as regards physical appearance should be wanting to bring glory to Christ and not draw attention to ourselves.

Discussion Starters

1. What helps you 'remain in the vine' (John 15:4–5)?

_____

_____

_____

_____

_____

2. What is the difference between the fruit of the Spirit and the gifts of the Spirit?

_____

_____

_____

_____

_____

3. What have you found helpful in dealing with an ongoing problem in your character where you don't seem to be making any headway?

_____

_____

_____

_____

_____

4. What does this phrase mean: 'men... to lift up holy hands in prayer, without anger or disputing'?

_____

_____

_____

_____

_____

5. How should we interpret 1 Timothy 2:9–10 for today's women?

_____

_____

_____

_____

_____

6. What challenges have you encountered when working in a secular workplace?

_____

_____

_____

_____

_____

7. What principles should guide us when faced with these challenges?

_____

_____

_____

_____

_____

8. In what ways could you enlarge your circle of non-Christian friends?

_____

_____

_____

_____

_____

Personal Application

'Walking the talk' encompasses our 'walk' – our behaviour towards others, and also our 'talk' – finding ways to share Christ with our friends, family and colleagues. Living an exemplary life before others without telling them of the power of God to do it will only discourage people. They'll think: he/she is such a good person, I could never be like that. It is far better to be open and honest about our faith in Christ even when we know our behaviour sometimes lets us down. Apologising for wrong behaviour gives people a glimpse of a God who forgives and accepts sinners.

It is much safer and cosier to spend the majority of our time with other believers, but this will result in God's people becoming more marginalised. We are called to be 'salt and light' – neither of which are any good if they are hidden away.

Decide on one practical action to take over the next month to develop your Christian character and also to develop your friendships with non-Christians.

Seeing Jesus in the Scriptures

Jesus 'went around doing good' (Acts 10:38). He had a wide circle of friends and acquaintances. People who'd been rejected by religious leaders felt at ease in His presence. He deftly bridged the gap between God and the world. He was creative in His approach using stories and illustrations people could relate to. His life backed up His message 100 per cent. The Holy Spirit indwells His people today to enable us to follow Christ's brilliant example.

WEEK 5

What Goes on at Church?

Opening Icebreaker

As a group make a list of the strengths and qualities you appreciate in the men and women who exercise leadership roles in your church.

Bible Readings

- 1 Timothy 1:1–2; 2:11–15; 5:1–2
- 1 Corinthians 2:3–5

Opening Our Eyes

Leaders called and equipped by God 1:1–2

Paul sometimes appears a confident leader. He bases
that on his call, not his ability. He knows himself to be
an 'apostle of Christ Jesus by the command of God
our Saviour and of Christ Jesus our hope'. Yet he also
acknowledges he felt weak and fearful when he came
to the Corinthians (1 Cor. 2:3–5). His confidence was that
God was using him to be a channel for the Spirit's power.
This would have encouraged Timothy. He too needed
to remember that God had called him, especially when
things weren't going so well.

Christian leaders need to have their confidence firmly
anchored in God's call. If He has asked you to fulfil
a role, then don't let anyone – human or demonic –
discourage you. He calls and He equips.

Women and their role 2:11–15

There are different interpretations of these verses. Sadly
they have sometimes been misused to silence dialogue.
As a background to looking at this passage let's review
some principles relating to interpreting the Bible: Look
at the passage within its context. Look for any other
passages which shed light on the subject. Take Scripture
as a unified whole. God will not contradict Himself.

Therefore it is not wise to build a doctrine on one or two
difficult verses.

Some of Paul's valued co-workers were women (Rom. 16).
In both the Jewish and Roman worlds women had
a low status, but Jesus changed all that. Paul also affirms
the value of each human being in Christ – 'all one in
Christ Jesus' (Gal. 3:26–29). So value is not in question

here – we are equal – the issue is role. How should women contribute their gifts and abilities to further God's kingdom?

Some say the Ephesian women were untaught and therefore needed to be still, to listen and learn before they could contribute. Untaught women, who were enjoying their new-found freedom in Christ, were possibly going over the top, asking questions or calling out in church gatherings, thus undermining the leaders. They needed to learn to be Christlike women and make their contribution in a Christlike way. The same is true today.

Paul's restriction on women teaching or having authority over men could therefore apply to untaught women. It is clear that women did pray and prophesy in public, so they were not all sitting silently (Acts 21:9; 1 Cor. 11:1–5).

Another tricky verse is 1 Timothy 2:15 which, if taken at face value, contradicts Paul's whole ethos which is 'salvation by faith alone'. It could mean (a) women finding fulfilment in motherhood; (b) women being saved through the birth of Christ; (c) women being kept safe in childbirth (NIV Study Bible).

Paul bases his teaching on male headship on the creation order (v13). He goes on to point out that Eve was deceived whereas Adam sinned with his eyes wide open (v14).

Church relationships 5:1–2

There are several pictures of church in the Bible. The one Paul uses here is family which encompasses respect, care and commitment.

Discussion Starters

1. What might have happened if Paul had doubted his calling?

2. In what ways does God call people to specific jobs?

3. What should a leader do if he/she hasn't got the gifts or abilities necessary to fulfil a required role?

4. In what ways did Jesus challenge the cultural attitude towards women?

5. What are some biblical examples of women having a significant role?

6. What principles should govern how a woman exercises her gifts in the church context?

_____

_____

_____

_____

7. What should a gifted woman do if she is in a situation where she cannot use her gifts?

_____

_____

_____

_____

8. What should characterise the church family?

_____

_____

_____

_____

9. How can we help other Christians feel valued?

_____

_____

_____

_____

10. What can you do to help your church work towards this ideal?

_____

_____

_____

_____

Personal Application

In a healthily functioning family there is room, encouragement and stimulus for everyone to develop to their full potential. In a dysfunctional family the members are more likely to receive criticism, lack of opportunity and discouragement to reach their potential.

God has graciously called, gifted and equipped men and women to serve in His family. There is much work to do and all are needed. It would be dreadful to meet God face to face and realise that we had been the cause of hindering some of His chosen people as they sought to fulfil His call on their lives.

Think about your attitude to both men and women leaders and potential leaders in the church. What can you do to help them along the way?

Seeing Jesus in the Scriptures

Jesus chose a very unlikely band to be His apostles. They responded to His call, went through His training programme and went on to change the world! They didn't always get everything right, but He didn't give up on them.

He encouraged women to listen to His teaching and welcomed them when they accompanied His group of disciples. He did all this in public, whereas it was forbidden for Jewish men to talk to a woman on the street, even if she were his wife, daughter or sister, let alone teach her Scripture! He radically challenged the prevailing negative attitude and affirmed the value of women. He wasn't threatened by women, but was secure in his own identity as a man.

WEEK 6

Wanted! Godly Leaders

Opening Icebreaker

Share about Christian leaders who have influenced you, either by their teaching, life or writing.

Bible Readings

- 1 Timothy 3:1–16; 5:17–25
- Matthew 23:1–12
- Mark 10:42–45

Opening Our Eyes

'Apathy is the acceptance of the unacceptable. Leadership begins with a decisive refusal to do so.' Thus writes John Stott in his book, *Issues Facing Christians Today*. He goes on to list five elements vital in leaders: clear vision, hard work, dogged perseverance, humble service and iron discipline. If you, in your church, want effective leaders, these would be crucial things to pray for them. If you are a leader, you could add these to your prayer list.

To aspire to exercise Christian leadership is truly 'a noble task' (3:1) and highly demanding. Those leaders who do well are 'worthy of double honour' (5:17). Honour should also include financial reward. Paul gives a fuller explanation of this in 1 Corinthians 9:7–14.

Part of Timothy's role in caring for the Ephesian church was to make sure it was properly led. A church cannot grow healthily if its leadership is unsound. Under a godly leader, the church will flourish. Paul, therefore, gives his young colleague clear practical guidance on character, gifts and skills needed in leaders.

Paul uses the terms 'overseer' and 'elder' interchangeably (Acts 20:17,28). Their role was to oversee the work of the church. Deacons (from Acts 6:1–7) were servants who assisted the elders. 'Their wives' in 3:11 simply means 'the women'. This could therefore mean deacons' wives, deaconesses or female deacons. Phoebe in Romans 16:1 is referred to as 'a servant of the church in Cenchrea'. 'Servant... when church related, as it is here, probably refers to a specific office – woman deacon or deaconess' (NIV Study Bible). What comes over from these verses is that ministry and life must go hand in hand. Stirring, eloquent, gifted preachers are so much wood, hay and stubble if their character does not live up to their words. Jesus reserves harsh criticism for the Pharisees in this regard (Matt. 23:1–12) – all outward religiosity but inner rottenness. The leader's home life and general reputation outside the church need to be consistent with the message.

Paul is referring in these verses to specific leadership roles, yet all Christians are called to serve in order to extend God's kingdom and, as such, all should aspire to this quality of life. Tragically, there are all too many cases where Christian leaders have fallen far short of this. Apart from causing sometimes irretrievable damage to their followers, the reputation of the Church has also taken a battering. This is where church discipline needs to be firmly exercised (1 Tim. 5:20).

The appointing of leaders is a serious affair, not to be rushed, but the result of careful, prayerful examination of proven candidates. God tested His potential leaders before giving them their responsibilities. Some examples are:

• Joseph served in Egypt for 13 years before becoming Pharaoh's chief of staff
• Moses looked after sheep for 40 years before taking on his mammoth task
• Joshua was Moses' assistant and proved his worth before taking over.

Once a leader or leadership team is in place it's tempting for the congregation to relax, sit back and expect great things to happen. But there are many pitfalls awaiting those who lead. The congregation has a vital responsibility to pray for their leaders so they will be protected from enemy attacks and walk in a way worthy of their calling.

Discussion Starters

1. What are the similarities between managing a household and managing a church?

2. What should be the priorities in the life of a church leader?

3. What happens if these priorities get out of synch?

4. How can a pastor build in some accountability for himself?

5. How can we encourage young people into leadership and at the same time make sure they are 'tested'.

6. What should the Church do to prepare future leaders?

_____

_____

_____

_____

7. What should an individual do to prepare him/herself for leadership?

_____

_____

_____

_____

8. If you were a pastor, what would be your dream congregation?

_____

_____

_____

_____

9. What can you do to become part of that dream team?

_____

_____

_____

_____

Personal Application

The Church needs godly gifted leaders. The leader's job is made infinitely more rewarding if the congregation or group is willing to respond to his/her leadership and grow in godliness and effective service (Heb. 13:17).

Wouldn't it be great if every church leader's work were a joy to him/her all the time? Wouldn't it be wonderful if every congregation benefited from the dynamic preaching, wise counsel and warm servant heart of its leader? However, we live in the real world. None of us will ever be the perfect leader or the ideal church member. But we can strive towards that goal, so that Christ's Body on earth will reflect something of His beauty.

What can you do towards that end? Think of one practical step you can take this week.

Seeing Jesus in the Scriptures

Jesus modelled servant leadership and impressed that upon His disciples (Mark 10:41–45). But being a servant leader did not mean being flabby or that He could be walked over. He insisted on high standards. Those who followed Him had to be willing to follow on His terms – total commitment (Mark 10:17–23; Luke 9:57–62).

Jesus displayed the five elements that John Stott brought out: clear vision, hard work, dogged perseverance, humble service and iron discipline. These, together with His sacrifical love and incomprehensible mercy, make Him the leader everyone should be proud and eager to follow no matter what the cost.

WEEK 7

Money, Money, Money!

Opening Icebreaker

Imagine you had David Beckham's income, how would you use it?

Share examples of how some rich people have used their wealth and how wealth has affected them.

Bible Readings

- 1 Timothy 5:3–16; 6:6–10,17–19
- Deuteronomy 8:10–20
- Luke 12:16–34
- Philippians 4:11–13

Opening Our Eyes

'Money, money, money... It's a rich man's world' –
thus went Abba's song. Well, it's God's world and He is
exceedingly rich! There is no one richer than He. What
does He do with all His wealth? He shares it around very
liberally (1 Tim. 6:17). But it does seem to be unequally
distributed. Topol in *Fiddler on the Roof* had a plaintive
conversation with the Almighty. 'Would it have spoilt
some vast eternal plan if I'd been a wealthy man?'

Many of us think we'd be very happy with just a small
fortune – enough to keep us comfortable. Then we read
ghastly statistics about world poverty (2.8 billion people
subsisting on less than $2 per day) and we realise that

most of us are already very comfortable.

In Timothy's time there was no State help for the poor,
and older widows were particularly vulnerable. There
seems to have been a system in the churches of putting
them on a list. These 'listed' widows had to be completely
alone with no family or other financial support. They
had to be of proven good character. There seems to have
been a reciprocal commitment. The church cared for them
and they devoted themselves to care for other church
members. It also seems that they made a commitment not
to remarry. Anna in Luke 2:36–37 would seem to have
been a precursor of this arrangement.

But the church couldn't care for every needy person. And
it is the same today. Resources are always finite. Families
in the church were urged to care for their own needy
relatives and consider this responsibility as a high priority.

Contentment seems to be a key (Phil. 4:11–13). The
dictionary defines 'being content' as: 'being pleased or
happy with what one has; satisfied.' So is it wrong to be

rich? Should wealthy people give away all they have? For some that might be necessary if materialism has entwined itself around their hearts so that their motivation is selfish. I'm not sure I could handle having vast sums of money, but there are very wealthy Christians who manage their money in a godly way for the benefit of God's kingdom. Contentment is a biblical imperative whether we are rich or poor.

The reality is that we are stewards of what God gives, and not owners (Deut. 8:18). We can't take it with us into the next world. We only have the use of it here on earth. We can do exciting things with it, investing it for God, or we can waste it (1 Tim. 6:17–19). Getting the right balance can be quite tricky. We can start feeling guilty about spending any money on ourselves, and then go the other way, and be over-indulgent.

I love the last phrase of 1 Timothy 6:17: 'God, who richly provides us with everything for our *enjoyment*' (my emphasis). God wants us to have a ball! 'Enjoy' is a recurring theme in Ecclesiastes (5:18–20; 9:7–10). Christians should be the happiest people on earth. As we walk with God we can use the money He gives us to meet the needs of others around us as well as to thoroughly enjoy ourselves.

Christians have sometimes had the reputation of never doing anything exciting. We are often more characterised by what we don't do, rather than what we do. We need to break that caricature, and use our resources to relish all that our generous God pours out on us.

Discussion Starters

1. Read Deuteronomy 8:10–20. What implications flow from this passage?

_____

_____

_____

_____

2. What lessons can be drawn from Luke 12:16–34?

_____

_____

_____

_____

3. How can we relate Jesus' teaching to our world where pensions and savings plans are considered vital?

_____

_____

_____

_____

4. Should Christians strive for promotion and higher salaries?

_____

_____

_____

_____

5. How is contentment shown in daily life?

_____

_____

_____

_____

6. What impact do you think contentment in the lives of Christians might have on the unbelieving world?

_____

_____

_____

_____

7. How can we resist greed and materialism?

_____

_____

_____

_____

8. Most of our governments give State help and overseas aid, so what is the individual Christian's responsibility towards the poor.

_____

_____

_____

_____

9. How can you bring your life more into line with these biblical imperatives?

_____

_____

_____

_____

Personal Application

Some people misquote 1 Timothy 6:10: 'money is the root of all evil', whereas it actually says 'the love of money is the root of all kinds of evil'. Money is a magnificent servant but a vicious master. We need to be in control of it and not allow it to dominate us in any way. Great and mighty wonders can be achieved with money. Lives can be changed. Christians can certainly put money to better use than the world can, so we need to take this superb servant that God has given us and use it to the full for Him. It follows then that it would be good to earn as much as possible and to put the money we have to the most efficient use.

In what ways do you need to rethink your convictions about money and possessions in order to be a wise steward?

Seeing Jesus in the Scriptures

Jesus, as a good Jewish boy, was taught a skill – carpentry. He earned his living at that until about age 30, so He was used to handling money. Then He gave up regular income, home comforts and financial independence and went on the road, dependent on others. His friends modelled sacrificial generosity that enabled Him to carry on His itinerant ministry. He knew what it was like to have to balance his budget and also live with financial insecurity. He displayed contentment and trust in His Father no matter what His financial situation. Let's follow His example.

Leader's Notes

Week 1: God is Listening

Opening Icebreaker

Write out promises about prayer on cards (some suggestions: Phil. 4:6,7; Jer. 33:3; Isa. 65:24; 2 Chron. 7:14; Matt. 21:22; Matt. 7:7; John 16:24; James 1:5–8).

Each group member should pick one and read it out.

The aim of the icebreaker is to get people used to speaking out in the group as well as laying the foundation for a growing confidence in prayer. You could prime a few people in the group to briefly share how they've experienced the truth of any of these promises.

Aim of the Session

To see the vital necessity of praise and prayer in our relationship with God, and to see ways of developing in both praise and prayer both privately and corporately.

If this is the first time your group has met, spend some moments first of all getting people to introduce themselves.

Encourage the group to read the whole letter through in one or two different versions and also the introduction in this chapter in their own time.

Discussion Starter 1: Faith grows as we see how fantastic Christ is. Try to tease out all the descriptions. An additional question could be: What does it mean to you that He is the King of kings and Lord of lords?

Discussion Starter 3: Through personal experience, knowledge of God's Word (2 Tim. 3:16) and the Spirit's help (John 14:26), Paul grew as a prayer giant, but he didn't start off that way. We don't reach a certain level and then ease off, what's important is to keep growing.

Discussion Starter 4: They gave him confidence to approach God and know that he would be heard (Eph. 3:12). They also gave him confidence in God's power to answer prayer (Heb. 4:14–16).

Discussion Starter 5: If any in the group are not sure whether or not they've accepted Christ, this would be a good opportunity to further explain the uniqueness of the Christian gospel. This is the only religion where God came down to take the place of sinful man so that we could be raised up and have access to God. In other religions man has to try to get to God through his own efforts. Without Christ God is unapproachable.

Discussion Starter 6: Paul opposed God and was forgiven. Peter denied Christ and was forgiven.

Discussion Starter 7: Some people pray persistently for weeks, months, even years for a situation. Sometimes God then impresses on their minds that there is no further need to pray. Instead they need to rest and leave the response to God. This is different to just getting discouraged because nothing seems to be happening. Ask different ones in the group what helps them to persist. A helpful biblical illustration is Elijah praying for rain in 1 Kings 18:42–46.

Discussion Starters 9 and 10: Out of these may come ideas for application. Try to help the group members to be realistic and practical. It is far better to start small, succeed and build on that, than have grandiose ideas and fall at the first hurdle. Reading Psalms, singing worship songs, looking at nature are fantastic prompts to praise; also, keeping a prayer diary and noting down requests and answers.

You might want to finish the discussion time with a prayer time. Be sensitive to those in the group who might not be used to praying aloud. One suggestion to help this would be to ask each person to think of one thing to praise God for and express that in just one sentence. You could go on to think about one thing to thank God for and again express it in one sentence.

Week 2: Watch Out! False Teachers About!

Opening Icebreaker

The aim is to alert people to examine what verses actually say and realise that a small adjustment can mean huge changes in meaning. It is easy to recognise when something is totally wrong. For example, if someone advocated child sacrifice we'd know they were off beam. But Satan is subtle. Some false teaching deviates only slightly from the truth, but will still lead people astray.

Aim of the Session

To alert people to the ever-present danger of being influenced by false teaching so we become more discerning about what we hear. To take practical steps to deepen in our knowledge and understanding of God's Word.

At the beginning of the study time, it would be helpful to reread the explanation in the Introduction of the false teachings attacking the Ephesian church in order to refresh people's minds. It would be good to remind

people that these false teachers were within the church context. It is easier to identify false teaching in outside groups, eg Jehovah's Witnesses, but some churches over- or under-emphasise some aspect of truth, and this can be very damaging. One example of this is the 'Protestant work ethic', where tireless work for the gospel is applauded. If workers are not also encouraged to obey the fourth commandment about resting on the Sabbath, burnout and disillusionment will be the result. Frenetic activity-filled lives are not attractive to those outside the Church.

Discussion Starter 2: Results include: controversies 1:4, meaningless talk 1:6 and lack of freedom 4:3. If these things are happening they represent warning lights that all is not well. Some people in the group may have personal examples of these.

Discussion Starter 3: If you have young Christians in the group they may be quite daunted to know there are dangerous heresies around but they need to be aware of them. Forewarned is forearmed.

Some examples:
• Prosperity gospel
• Practising homosexuals in church leadership
• Living a good life is all that's required
• God wants me to be happy so I can just do what makes me happy
• New Age stuff – crystals, etc.

Discussion Starter 4: John 8:44 is a useful cross-reference. In identifying Satan and his demons as the source, you can be encouraged that 'the one who is in you is greater than the one who is in the world' (1 John 4:4). We don't fight Satan and his demons in our own strength but trust in the victory that Jesus won on the cross.

Discussion Starter 6:

- Growing in our knowledge of God's Word through listening to sermons, talks, participating in Bible studies, reading and meditating on Scripture. The leader could have some resources available for the group members to consider – eg some daily devotional reading books, Bible study books, correspondence courses, Bible memory verses.
- Meeting with other Bible-believing Christians.
- Praying for discernment and the Holy Spirit's help.
- Being aware of the dangers.

Discussion Starter 8:

- Affirming what we do agree on
- Accepting others' differences – agreeing to differ while maintaining the relationship. In some cases of doctrinal disagreement this may involve deciding to leave one fellowship and worship elsewhere. But we should always seek to discuss our differences with respect and Christian love.
- Seeking not to be a stumbling block, ie using our freedom without regard for others' scruples; 1 Corinthians 8 has some illuminating insights on this topic.

At the end of the discussion time one suggestion would be to review the aims of the study and ask each person to select one practical thing they can do over the next few weeks to deepen in their knowledge of God's Word.

Week 3: Use Your Gifts

Opening Icebreaker

The aim is to refresh people's minds about what the spiritual gifts are and how to identify them in use.

Aim of the Session

To see the importance of identifying and using our spiritual gifts to the full for God's glory. To take steps in this area.

It would be wise not to get sidetracked in helping people identify their gifts during the discussion time. It would be better to concentrate on the study and leave the issue of people's specific gifts for later.

Discussion Starter 1: The aim of this question is to see the broad scope of the role Timothy was to fill and just what a challenge it would have been for him.

Discussion Starter 2: Even though Timothy had learned a lot from being alongside Paul in ministry, Paul had always been the leader, and now Timothy had to take the load alone. A useful cross-reference is Philippians 2:19–23 where Paul praises Timothy for his genuine pastoral heart. Timothy was called by God and gifted by God. He'd received on-the-job training and experience in other cities, but what was equally important, was his deep genuine concern and care for people. Gifts and call need to be backed up by character.

Discussion Starter 3: Being undermined by criticism because of his youth might well have discouraged him. Some might well have compared him to Paul which would also have proved difficult, as well as the more obvious battles of dealing with false teachers.

Discussion Starter 4: In this question you could go on to ask the group members what has helped them persevere in pursuing God's call for them despite difficult circumstances.

Discussion Starter 5: It would be good to remind the group members that gifts are not given in a fully developed state. Timothy's gifts became apparent as he served, as well as through prophetic words and the affirmation of other leaders like Paul.

Discussion Starter 6:
- Gifts are given for the common good (1 Cor. 12:7)
- The aim is to bring praise to God (1 Pet. 4:10,11)
- 'So that the Body of Christ may be built up' (Eph. 4:1–12)

Discussion Starter 7: For this question it would be good to read the parable of the talents in Matthew 25:14–30.

Discussion Starter 8: Try to help the group make specific plans to follow through on this study. Some may have no idea of their gifting, and need a basic programme to identify them. Others may just need some prompting to get involved in some ministry and see what God develops in them. Others may know their gifts but possibly need some stimulus to develop and use them in a broader sphere of service.

It would be good to recap at the end of the group time the exhortation in 1 Timothy 4:16: 'Watch your life and your doctrine closely.' Along with developing our gifts, we need to develop a Christlike character and a close walk with God, so that our gifts are used with the best possible motivation.

Week 4: Walk the Talk

Opening Icebreaker

The words love, joy, peace, etc., can trip off the tongue quite easily. The aim of this icebreaker is to broaden understanding of what these words encompass. Try not to let this take too long – just give about 30 seconds to write down their first thought. If they can't think of anything, move on to the next one. Some responses may be quite light-hearted, others more serious.

Sharing briefly with each other at the end should give a fuller appreciation of these qualities.

Aim of the Session

To challenge each one to live an authentic Christian life and to make a specific commitment to grow in some aspect of Christian character and in reaching out to non-Christians.

Discussion Starter 1: Regular devotional life is probably the number one priority here. It would be good to have some examples of devotional Bible reading notes to show people, eg *Every Day with Jesus, Inspiring Women Every Day, Life Every Day* (Jeff Lucas) or *Cover to Cover Every Day* (all CWR). This might help them get started if they are not already having some time with God each day. A supplementary question here would be to ask others in the group what they do for their quiet time. You could possibly pair the group members up to arrange a special time to have a quiet time together.

Other helps include: meeting with other Christians for encouragement and stimulus, and openness to the Holy Spirit's guidance throughout the day.

Discussion Starter 2: All the fruit is for all Christians and grows slowly through experience of walking with God. One or more gifts are given to individual Christians for specific roles. This subject is dealt with more fully in the chapter: 'Use your Gifts'.

Discussion Starter 3: Resist discouragement. Celebrate small successes. Ask others to pray with you.

Some situations may require specific prayer to break Satanic strongholds. Some issues have unforgiveness at the root – this needs to be identified and repented of.

Keep close to the Vine.

Discussion Starter 4: A helpful cross-reference here is Psalm 66:16–20.

Discussion Starter 5: There is a balance here between not being so conservative in dress that Christian women appear odd, and not conforming slavishly to fashion or being immodest. This could provoke some lively discussion especially among younger women. It's important to stress the underlying attitude of not dressing to attract attention to oneself, but to reflect some beautiful aspect of God. You might want to widen this out to include how the men dress!

Discussion Starter 6: Challenges to integrity and honesty:
• Using the employer's resources – telephone, stationery, time off sick, leaving early, arriving late, etc.
• Some employers demand too much – longer and longer hours of stress-filled work.
• Difficult customers, awkward workmates.
• Gossip, criticism, dirty jokes, blasphemy, excluding some colleagues because they are different in some way.

Discussion Starter 7: Some helpful principles:
- Think – What would Jesus do?
- My employer is God – He wants me to be a light here.
- If intolerable, pray and look for another job – it's better to have a smaller salary and sanity than to be worked to death and neglect other responsibilities.
- Prayer.

Discussion Starter 8: It would be good to draw out from the group what they have tried – some suggestions could be sports or special interest clubs, evening classes, neighbours. Some may say they haven't got the time or energy to be involved with any more people. It would be good to help them think through on the balance of their Christian and non-Christian friends. In order to free up some time it might mean reducing church activities.

At the end give time for each one to come up with a clear plan of how they are going to respond to the question in Personal Application.

Week 5: What Goes on at Church?

Opening Icebreaker

This icebreaker is aimed at focusing on the positive aspects of leaders in your church or group. You, as the leader, must be quick to steer the group away from any negative comments.

Aim of the Session

To gain a clearer understanding of men and women's roles within the Church and to see ways of developing closer relationships within the church family.

This study could lead to some lively discussion as many people have entrenched views on the role of women. It would be good to urge the group members to pray for open, teachable hearts, and sensitivity and patience towards each other which would involve really listening to what others are saying. The chapter entitled 'Women, Men and God' in John Stott's book, *Issues Facing Christians Today* (Marshall Pickering, 1990) gives an extensive overview of different viewpoints and discussion. He poses an interesting question: 'So is it possible whether... the requirement of "silence"... was not an absolute prohibition of women teaching men, but rather a prohibition of every kind of teaching by women which attempts to reverse sexual roles and even domineer over men?' He considers the answer to be 'Yes'.

Discussion Starter 3: Some leaders feel they need to do everything, as many a congregation knows to its cost. Leaders need to be given the freedom to refuse a particular role, or bring someone else along to do it. If no one else is available, they should be earnest in prayer that God would give them the necessary gift or raise someone else up for it.

Discussion Starter 4: It is important to stress how radical Jesus' attitude was for His time.

- He encouraged Mary to listen to His teaching rather than be in the 'proper' place for her culturally (Luke 10:38–42).
- He announced His resurrection to a woman, whereas culturally women were not considered reliable witnesses.
- He spoke to a women at Jacob's well – a woman, Samaritan and a sinner – three counts against her (John 4:1–26).
- He allowed a prostitute to wet His feet with her tears and wipe them with her hair – He accepted her love (Luke 7:36–50).
- He allowed them to accompany Him on His travels (Luke 8:1–3).

Discussion Starter 5: Some examples are: Hannah, Deborah, Mary (mother of Jesus), Priscilla, Dorcas (Rom. 16: Phoebe, Junias, Tryphena, Tryphose, Persis, Rufus' mother), Esther, Anna.

Discussion Starter 6: Some discussion of 'male headship' would be useful here. This topic is also covered well by John Stott in *Issues Facing Christians Today*. He stresses that male headship is not designed to allow men to dominate, nor does it imply inferiority. Rather it is the 'God-given means by which their womanhood is respected, protected and enabled to blossom'. Also 'it would be more conducive to the full flowering of their womanhood if... they could experience the respect and supportive care of a man or men' (pp273–274).

This has huge implications. For men... to be the kind of man who enables the full flowering of womanhood by being respectful and supportive. For women, especially single women, to work towards cultivating respectful and supportive friendships with men in a non-threatening manner, not seeking to reverse the roles.

Discussion Starter 9: A supplementary question would be: What helps you feel valued? Some possible responses:
• Affirm and give people opportunities to use their gifts
• Ask their opinion
• Listen to them
• Appreciate what they do – flowers, service, teaching
• Notice when they are not there.

It would be good to really work on some practical application of this study, particularly if divergent views have been expressed. You could focus on Discussion Starter 10 and help people come up with specific practical things they can work on over the following few weeks.

If you sense that people are upset or disturbed by the discussion, acknowledge this and take some time to pray at the end of the discussion time for people to forgive one another and respect their viewpoints.

Week 6: Wanted! Godly Leaders

Aim of the Session

To gain a clearer picture of the qualities needed in a leader. To take steps to go deeper in praying for and supporting leaders, and/or becoming a more effective and godly leader.

It might be necessary at the beginning of this study to point out to the group that this is not the time to dwell on the imperfections of their church leaders! If there are current difficulties with the church leadership it would be wise to pray briefly for the leaders. Then it would be good to encourage the group to focus on what Scripture says and seek to learn from God.

Some group members may sit back and think that this topic does not concern them as they think they will never become leaders. Encourage them to see that the qualities of character are equally important for church members as for the leaders.

Discussion Starter 2: The priorities are: 1. God; 2. Close family; 3. Church and possibly part-time job; 4. Friends and wider family.

Discussion Starter 3: Very often the demands of leadership are such that church becomes priority number one. The leader's devotional life and family life suffer as a result. The leader then becomes 'dry' spiritually. The family feels neglected; the church will not flourish. Another result can be that if the leader is doing too much of the work of the church, the congregation can tend to rely too heavily on him/her and is not mobilised into action. They sit back and watch their pastor get more and more exhausted.

A supplementary question on this topic could be: What can you do to help the pastor maintain the right priorities? Some possible suggestions: don't phone him on his day off; direct your queries to the appropriate person, not always at the pastor; suggest the church pays for him/her to go on a spiritual retreat.

Discussion Starters 5 and 6: There is definitely a leadership gift, but people need to grow into that. Giving people small responsibilities enables their gift to be identified and developed.

It's important when giving people responsibility to not just dump it on them and abandon them to get on with it. The art of delegation is to make sure people understand what is expected of them and to give clear accountability lines. People also need support when taking on a new responsibility. It is helpful to have a time limit, for example one or two years, rather than people feeling they are stuck with this new task forever.

All of us when taking on any new role need lots of encouragement and positive feedback. We need to be honest with each other and, in love, share possible areas of needed development.

Discussion Starters 8 and 9: A dream congregation:
- Enthusiastic
- Worshipful
- Welcoming
- Supportive
- Encouraging
- Volunteering
- Honest, not gossiping, or critical

If there were a problem they would try to sort it out in the attitude of keeping 'the unity of the Spirit through the bond of peace' (Eph. 4:3).

At the end of the study, each group member should identify one practical thing they could do to put these Scriptures into practice. You could finish by praying over these things and also praying for the church leaders.

Week 7: Money, Money, Money!

Opening Icebreaker

It would be good to have some positive and negative examples of the way people have used money and its effect on them. To summarise the Icebreaker you could give the example of John Wesley – the founder of the Methodist movement. He operated his finances on the basis of his needs and not his income. He determined that he needed £28 per year and he gave the rest away. Even when his income went up significantly, he still maintained his own needs at £28. Obviously he lived in a time of nil inflation, but the principle is still a good one.

For many of us today as our income goes up so does our standard of living. We operate on the basis of income and not needs. Do our needs really expand, or are we just indulging ourselves?

Aim of the Session

To give a broader understanding of the value and pitfalls of money and possessions.

To promote practical application of these principles in daily life.

This topic can be controversial. We are often quite quick to comment on the way other people use money, but not so keen to put the spotlight on ourselves.

Discussion Starter 1: Implications:
• Thankfulness for all that God has given
• Recognising He is the Giver
• Financial security can cause us to be lukewarm in our faith – when we are needy we cry out to Him; when all is well, we forget
• Recognise that He enables us to produce wealth – the gifts and abilities are His.

Discussion Starter 4: Christians have a responsibility to fully use all the gifts and abilities that God has given. Striving for excellence in the workplace honours God, and this is sometimes reflected in monetary terms. It's what we do with the money that is important, not how much we earn. This does need to be balanced with other areas of life, eg not spending so much time and energy at work that we neglect our families, or living an unbalanced life with no time for fun.

Discussion Starter 5: Contentment is shown by thankfulness and enjoyment of life. You could discuss in the group what helps them enjoy life, especially if it doesn't involve a huge expense. Not complaining about low salary, or increasing cost of living also reveals contentment, as well as not craving, envying or buying more possessions when you already have sufficient.

Discussion Starter 7: By remembering that many people go to bed hungry, their children don't go to school, they have no health care and often don't know where the next meal is coming from.

It is also helpful not to place oneself in situations of temptation – eg window shopping, watching the ads on TV. One can very quickly go from, 'That's nice' to 'I would like that' to 'I must have it'.

Discussion Starter 8: Some in the group may feel overwhelmed with the constant plea for money by different charities. The stories are heartbreaking and the needs seem too great. One can be on a constant guilt trip. We need to realise that we cannot meet every need nor does God expect us to. It's helpful at the beginning of the year to pray through one's financial situation and decide which charities/church ministries to support and then one can, with a clear conscience, put all the other requests in the bin!

Notes...

SmallGroup central

All of our small group ideas and resources in one place

Online:

www.smallgroupcentral.org.uk
is filled with free video teaching, tools, articles and a whole host of ideas.

On the road:

A range of seminars themed for small groups can be brought to your local community. Contact us at **hello@smallgroupcentral.org.uk**

In print:

Books, study guides and DVDs covering an extensive list of themes, Bible books and life issues.

Log on and find out more at:
www.smallgroupcentral.org.uk

Be inspired by God.
Every day.

COVER TO COVER | EVERY **DAY**
JAN/FEB 2017

Genesis 12–50
John 12–21

Bringing you deeper biblical understanding | CWR

Cover to Cover Every Day

In-depth study of the Bible, book by book. Part of a five-year series. Available as an email subscription or on eBook and Kindle.

One-year subscriptions available for all titles

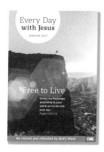

Every Day with Jesus

The popular daily Bible reading notes by Selwyn Hughes.

Inspiring Women Every Day

Daily insight and encouragement written by women for women.

Life Every Day

Lively Bible notes, with Jeff Lucas' wit and wisdom.

To order or subscribe, visit **www.cwr.org.uk/store** or call **01252 784700**.
Also available in Christian bookshops.

 Print subscription available

 **Large Print subscription** available

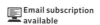 **Email subscription** available

The bestselling *Cover to Cover* Bible Study Series

1 Corinthians
Growing a Spirit-filled church
ISBN: 978-1-85345-374-8

2 Corinthians
Restoring harmony
ISBN: 978-1-85345-551-3

1 Peter
Good reasons for hope
ISBN: 978-1-78259-088-0

2 Peter
Living in the light of God's promises
ISBN: 978-1-78259-403-1

1 Timothy
*Healthy churches –
effective Christians*
ISBN: 978-1-85345-291-8

23rd Psalm
The Lord is my shepherd
ISBN: 978-1-85345-449-3

2 Timothy and Titus
Vital Christianity
ISBN: 978-1-85345-338-0

Abraham
Adventures of faith
ISBN: 978-1-78259-089-7

Acts 1-12
Church on the move
ISBN: 978-1-85345-574-2

Acts 13-28
To the ends of the earth
ISBN: 978-1-85345-592-6

Barnabas
Son of encouragement
ISBN: 978-1-85345-911-5

Bible Genres
Hearing what the Bible really says
ISBN: 978-1-85345-987-0

Daniel
Living boldly for God
ISBN: 978-1-85345-986-3

David
A man after God's own heart
ISBN: 978-1-78259-444-4

Ecclesiastes
*Hard questions and
spiritual answers*
ISBN: 978-1-85345-371-7

Elijah
A man and his God
ISBN: 978-1-85345-575-9

Elisha
A lesson in faithfulness
ISBN: 978-1-78259-494-9

Ephesians
Claiming your inheritance
ISBN: 978-1-85345-229-1

Esther
For such a time as this
ISBN: 978-1-85345-511-7

Fruit of the Spirit
Growing more like Jesus
ISBN: 978-1-85345-375-5

Galatians
Freedom in Christ
ISBN: 978-1-85345-648-0

God's Rescue Plan
*Finding God's fingerprints
on human history*
ISBN: 978-1-85345-294-9

Great Prayers of the Bible
Applying them to our lives toda
ISBN: 978-1-85345-253-6

Hebrews
Jesus – simply the best
ISBN: 978-1-85345-337-3

For current prices or to order, visit **www.cwr.org.uk/store**
Available online or from Christian bookshops.

Courses and events

Waverley Abbey College

Publishing and media

Conference facilities

Transforming lives

N.J.

CWR's vision is to enable people to experience
personal transformation through applying God's Word
to their lives and relationships.

Our Bible-based training and resources help people
around the world to:
• Grow in their walk with God
• Understand and apply Scripture to their lives
• Resource themselves and their church
• Develop pastoral care and counselling skills
• Train for leadership
• Strengthen relationships, marriage and family life
and much more.

CWR Applying God's Word
to everyday life and relationships

CWR, Waverley Abbey House,
Waverley Lane, Farnham,
Surrey GU9 8EP, UK

Telephone: **+44 (0)1252 784700**
Email: **info@cwr.org.uk**
Website: **www.cwr.org.uk**

Registered Charity No. 294387
Company Registration No. 1990308

Our insightful writers provide daily Bible reading
notes and other resources for all ages, and our
experienced course designers and presenters have
gained an international reputation for excellence and
effectiveness.

CWR's Training and Conference Centres in Surrey
and East Sussex, England, provide excellent facilities
in idyllic settings – ideal for both learning and spiritu
refreshment.